Spark.
words and pictures for activating English

WORKBOOK
4

Name:	_____
Class:	_____
Address:	_____
	_____
Phone:	_____

Beth Haynes

ACTUAL

Copyright © Beth Haynes 2003
Text, Design and Illustration Actual Enterprises 2003
First published 2003
Printed in Australia by Southwood Press

Acknowledgements

While every care has been taken to trace and acknowledge copyright, the publishers tender their apologies for any accidental infringement.

Copying for educational purposes

The **Australian Copyright Act 1968** (the Act) allows a maximum of one chapter or 10% of this book, whichever is the greater, to be copied by any educational institution for its educational purposes provided that that educational institution (or the body that administers it) has given a remuneration notice to Copyright Agency Limited (CAL) under the Act.

For details of the CAL licence for educational institutions contact CAL, tel (02) 9394 7600, fax (02) 9394 7601, email info@copyright.com.au

Copying for other purposes

Except as permitted under the Act (for example any fair dealing for the purposes of study, research, criticism or review) no part of this book may be reproduced, stored in a retrieval system, or transmitted in any form or by any means without prior written permission. All inquiries should be made to the publisher at the address below.

ISBN 0-9750208-2-X

Actual Enterprises
PO Box 14 Glebe 2037
spark@actual.com.au
www.actual.com.au

Message for Students:

★ The **Spark Wordbank** and **Workbooks** will help you improve your English.

★ The **Wordbank** will teach you the most important words. You can look through the book to check words you need, or use the Contents or Index. You can use it for school lessons or at home.

★ The **Workbooks** build from the language in the **Wordbank** to develop your understanding. The **Workbooks** will help you with reading, writing, speaking, listening and viewing. They will also help you understand the language of classroom instructions. You can work with your teacher, by yourself, with your classmates, and at home.

★ You will enjoy improving day by day. By the time you have completed these books, your English will be much better and you will feel much stronger! Then you'll be ready for the next stage in your learning. Good luck!

Contents

Feelings 5-9
Favourites 10-13
Classifying 14, 15
Things at School 16-22
The Weather 23-31
Family 32-42
Dates 43, 44
Opinions 45-51
The House and Bedroom . . 52-57
Opposites 58-62
Places 63-67
Address 68, 69
Forms and Envelope 70, 71
Directions 72-80
Places in Australia 81, 82
The Solar System 83, 84
Lily Was Lucky! 85-93
Shopping Game 94, 95

Feelings (1)

How do they feel?
Find Feelings in 'Spark Wordbank.'
Write the names of the feelings under the pictures.

spark workbook 4

Feelings (2)

Write the names of the feelings.
Also choose the correct endings for the sentences.

➡ 1. I feel _____ when _____.

2. I feel _____ when _____.

3. I feel _____ when _____.

4. I feel _____ when _____.

5. I feel _____ when _____.

6. I feel _____ when _____.

▸ I go swimming in winter
▸ I go to the library
▸ I go to my friend's house
▸ I eat too much food
▸ I listen to sad music
▸ I go to the beach in summer

Feelings (3)

Continue making the sentences.

7. I feel _____ when _____.

8. I feel _____ when _____.

9. I feel _____ when _____.

10. I feel _____ when _____.

11. I feel _____ when _____.

12. I feel _____ when _____.

- ▶ *I sit in the garden*
- ▶ *someone wants to fight with me*
- ▶ *I meet some new people*
- ▶ *I need some water*
- ▶ *the schoolwork is too difficult*
- ▶ *I need some food*

spark workbook 4

Feelings (4)

Continue making the sentences.

13. I feel _____ when _____.

14. I feel _____ when _____.

15. I feel _____ when _____.

16. I feel _____ when _____.

17. I feel _____ when _____.

18. I feel _____ when _____.

- ▶ *I go on a picnic*
- ▶ *I do nothing*
- ▶ *I hear a loud noise*
- ▶ *I see a horror movie*
- ▶ *I'm late for school*
- ▶ *I stay awake late at night*

Feelings (5)

How do you feel?
Copy the sentences from the last three pages.

➡ 1. <u>I feel happy when</u>

2.

3.
4.
5.

6.
7.
8.

9.
10.

11.
12.
13.
14.
15.
16.
17.
18.

Favourites (1)

What do you like the best?

Find these topics in 'Spark Wordbank.'
Write down the page numbers and your favourites.

	TOPIC	PAGE NUMBERS	MY FAVOURITE...
1.	place	6-9	
2.	colour		
3.	clothing		
4.	activity	24-29	
5.	sport		
6.	food		
7.	animal		
8.	room in the house		
9.	season		
10.	time of the day		
11.	day of the week		
12.	music		

page 10

spark workbook 4

Favourites (2)

Write sentences about your favourites.
▶ My favourite _place_ is _the park_ .
Also make extra sentences.

1. ___
2. ___
3. ___
4. ___
5. ___
6. ___
7. ___
8. ___
9. ___
10. ___
11. ___
12. ___
13. ___
14. ___
15. ___
16. ___
17. ___
18. ___

Favourites (3)

▶ What is your favourite _place_ ?
Write the topics in the left-hand column.
Ask your classmates and write their answers.

TOPIC / NAME					
1. place					
2.					
3.					
4.					
5.					
6.					
7.					
8.					
9.					
10.					
11.					
12.					

Favourites (4)

Write one or more sentences about some of your classmates' favourites.

▶ _Kim's_ favourite _food_ is _watermelon_ .

1.
2.
3.
4.
5.
6.
7.
8.
9.
10.
11.
12.
13.
14.
15.
16.
17.
18.
19.
20.
21.
22.
23.

Classifying (1)

Which topics do these words belong to?
Write the words on this page in the correct spaces on the next page.

Tuesday	football	yellow
rice	jacket	dog
drum	summer	tee-shirt
park	green	tennis
morning	getting a letter	kitchen
guitar	beach	winter
Thursday	elephant	apple
cricket	afternoon	talking
brown	didgeridoo	school
hat	bedroom	Friday
night	jumper	spring
cat	piano	playing a game
collecting cards	basketball	river
kangaroo	soup	autumn
lounge-room	Sunday	orange

Classifying (2)

 Which topics do the items belong to? Classify the words from the last page into the correct spaces on this page.

	TOPIC	ITEMS
1.	place	park - river -
2.	colour	
3.	clothing	
4.	activity	
5.	sport	
6.	food	
7.	animal	
8.	room in the house	
9.	season	
10.	time of the day	
11.	day of the week	
12.	music	

Things at School (1)

What are they called?
What is it called? What is this called?
Write the names under the pictures.

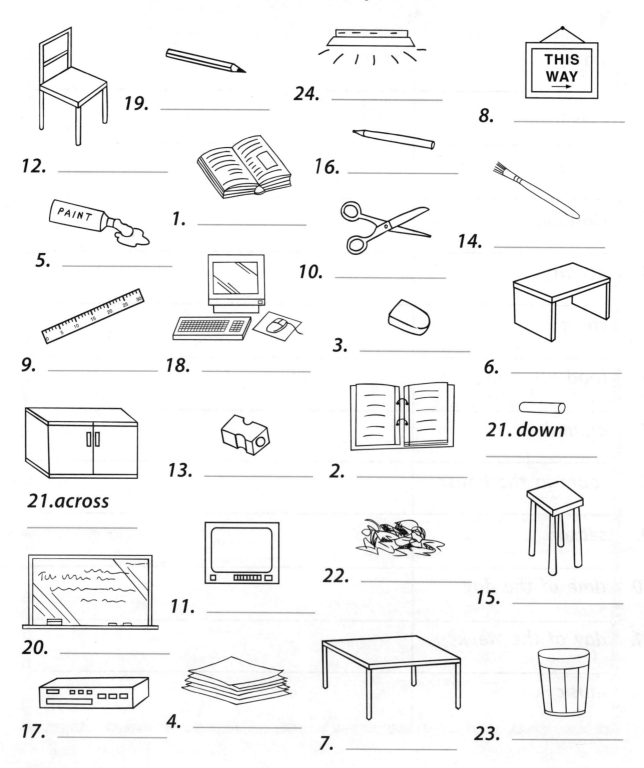

Things at School (2)

Crossword Puzzle
Now write the words onto the crossword puzzle.
They go ACROSS and DOWN.

spark workbook 4

page 17

Things at School (3)

What are they?
What is it?
Write the names of the objects.

1. It is big, has 4 legs and you sit at it. _____
2. It is medium-sized and you sit at it. _____
3. It is medium-sized, has 4 legs and you sit on it.

   _____
4. It is very small and you sharpen your pencil with it.

   _____   _____
5. It is small, long and thin, and you paint with it.

   _____
6. It is small or medium-sized, and you turn it on to see everything better. _____
7. It is big or small, has writing on it and tells you something. _____
8. It is big or small, and you put it in the bin.

   _____
9. It is big with doors and you keep things inside it.

   _____
10. It is medium-sized, uses electricity and you can watch TV shows on it. _____

Things at School (4)

What are they like?
What is it like?
Make new sentences from the last sentences.

▶ A <u>table</u> is <u>big, has 4 legs and you sit at it.</u>

1. A table is
2.
3.
4.
5.
6.
7.
8. Rubbish is
9.
10.

spark workbook 4   page 19

Things at School (5)

 Join the beginnings of the definitions with the endings.

1. A book is small, made of paper	and you write or draw with it.
2. A ruler is long and thin	and you cut paper with them.
3. A pencil is small, long and thin	and you rub out mistakes with it.
4. A pen is small, long and thin	and you rule lines with it.
5. The board is big	and you write with it.
6. Scissors are small	and the teacher writes on it.
7. A rubber is very small	and you write on the board with it.
8. Chalk is very small	and you read it.

 Now write the definitions.

➡ 1. *A book is small, made of paper and you read it.*
2. _____
3. _____
4. _____
5. _____
6. _____
7. _____
8. _____

page 20   spark workbook 4

Things at School (6)A

Do it! Student A:
Read the instructions with your partner (Student B on the next page). Write the missing words.

➡ 1. Turn on the light.
➡ 2. Put the rubbish in the _____.
3. Sit on the chair.
4. Sit at the _____.
5. Watch TV.
6. Watch a _____.
7. Open your folder.
8. Read a _____.
9. Read the sign.
10. Pick up the _____.
11. Put the scissors in the cupboard.
12. Rule a line with the _____.
13. Turn on the computer.
14. Take out a piece of _____.
15. Look at the writing on the board.
16. Colour the picture with coloured _____.
17. Write with a pen.
18. Cut the paper with _____.
19. Paint a picture with a paintbrush and paint.
20. Sharpen the pencil with a _____ _____.
21. Write on the board with chalk.
22. Rub out the mistake with a _____.
23. Put the stool next to the _____.

spark workbook 4   page 21

Things at School (6)B

Do it! Student B:
Read the instructions with your partner (Student A on the last page). Write the missing words.

➡ 1. Turn on the _____.
➡ 2. Put the rubbish in the bin.
3. Sit on the _____.
4. Sit at the desk.
5. Watch _____.
6. Watch a video.
7. Open your _____.
8. Read a book.
9. Read the _____.
10. Pick up the rubbish.
11. Put the scissors in the _____.
12. Rule a line with the ruler.
13. Turn on the _____.
14. Take out a piece of paper.
15. Look at the writing on the _____.
16. Colour the picture with coloured pencils.
17. Write with a _____.
18. Cut the paper with scissors.
19. Paint a picture with a _____ and _____.
20. Sharpen the pencil with a pencil sharpener.
21. Write on the board with _____.
22. Rub out the mistake with a rubber.
23. Put the _____ next to the table.

The Weather (1)A

Student A:
Read this conversation with your partner and write the missing words.

Hi! How are you?

_____! Good, _____. How _____ you?

Good, thanks. What's the weather like today?

It's _____ and _____.

Do you like this weather?

Yes, I _____ it.

What do you like to do on a warm day?

I like _____ go _____ and to _____ to _____ park.

What clothes do you like to wear on a warm day?

I like to _____ a _____ and _____.

spark workbook 4 page 23

The Weather (1)B

Student B:
Read this conversation with your partner and write the missing words.

B: Hi! How _____ you?

A: Hello! Good, thanks. How about you?

B: _____, thanks. What's _____ weather like _____?

A: It's warm and sunny.

B: Do _____ like this _____?

A: Yes, I like it.

B: What _____ you like to _____ on a warm _____?

A: I like to go swimming and to go to the park.

B: What _____ do you _____ to wear _____ a _____ day?

A: I like to wear a tee-shirt and jeans.

The Weather (2)

 First copy the questions.
Then ask your partner about the real weather today.
After that, write your partner's answers.

The Weather (3)

What is the weather like today?

Fill in the missing words.
(Notice the different word endings.)

___   _____   _____   _____

_____   _____   _____   ____

➡ 1. It is a ☀ **sunny** day.

2. It is a ☁ **cloudy** day.

3. It is a 🌧 _____ day.

4. It is a 💨 _____ day.

5. It is a 💨 ____**zy** day.

6. It is a ⛈ _____ day.

7. It is a ☀ ____**d** day. It is ☀ **very hot**.

8. It is ❄ ____**ing** today. It is ❄ ____ ____.

page 26   spark workbook 4

The Weather (4)

 A Stormy Day
Fill in the missing words.

➡ 1. It is a _____ day. There are _____s, ____, and ____. There is _____ and _____.

 How hot or cold is it?

➡ 1. It is _very hot_.
2. It is ___.
3. It is _____.
4. It is ____.
5. It is ____.
6. It is ____.
7. It is ____ ____.

Weather Chart (1)

 What was the weather like?
Write the correct words under the pictures.

	hot or cold	sunny or cloudy	rainy or fine	windy or calm
Monday	very cold			calm
Tuesday				
Wednesday				
Thursday				
Friday				
Saturday				
Sunday				

page 28 spark workbook 4

Weather Chart (2)

Write sentences about the weather chart.
▶ **On** <u>Monday</u>, **it was** <u>very cold</u>, <u>cloudy</u>, <u>rainy</u> **and** <u>calm</u>.

1. On Monday, it was _____, _____, _____ and _____.

2. On Tuesday, it was _____, _____, _____ and _____.

3. On _____, it was _____, _____, _____ and _____.

4. On _____, it was _____, _____, _____ and _____.

5. On, _____

6. _____

7. _____

spark workbook 4 page 29

Weather Chart (3)

What will the weather be like this week?

Make a weather chart each day for this week.

	hot or cold	sunny or cloudy	rainy or fine	windy or calm
Monday				
Tuesday				
Wednesday				
Thursday				
Friday				
Saturday				
Sunday				

Weather Chart (4)

What was the weather like?

After you have completed the weather chart, make sentences describing the weather.

▶ On _Monday_ , it was _____ , _____ , _____ and _____ .

1. _____

2. _____

3. _____

4. _____

5. _____

6. _____

7. _____

Family (1)

Robin Lee's Family Tree

Label the Lee family tree from Robin Lee's point of view.

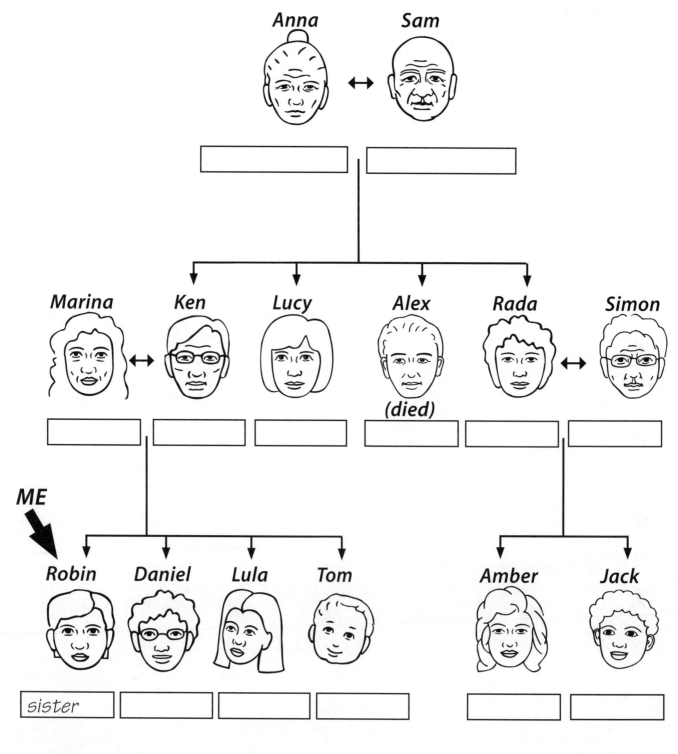

page 32   spark workbook 4

Family (2)

Robin Lee's Family Tree

Fill in the missing words about the Lee family tree, from Robin Lee's point of view.

1. This is the Lee family.
➡ 2. My name is *Robin*.
3. I've got a sister called _____.
4. I've also got two brothers called _____ and _____.
5. I've got two cousins - a girl called _____ and a boy called _____.
6. Mum's name is _____ and Dad's name is _____.
7. I've got an aunt called _____.
8. I've got an uncle called _____. He died five years ago.
9. There's also Aunt _____ who is married to Uncle _____.
10. My grandmother on my father's side is called _____ and my grandfather is called _____.
11. My grandparents on my mother's side both died.

spark workbook 4

Family (3)

Sam Lee's Family Tree
Label the family tree from Sam Lee's point of view.

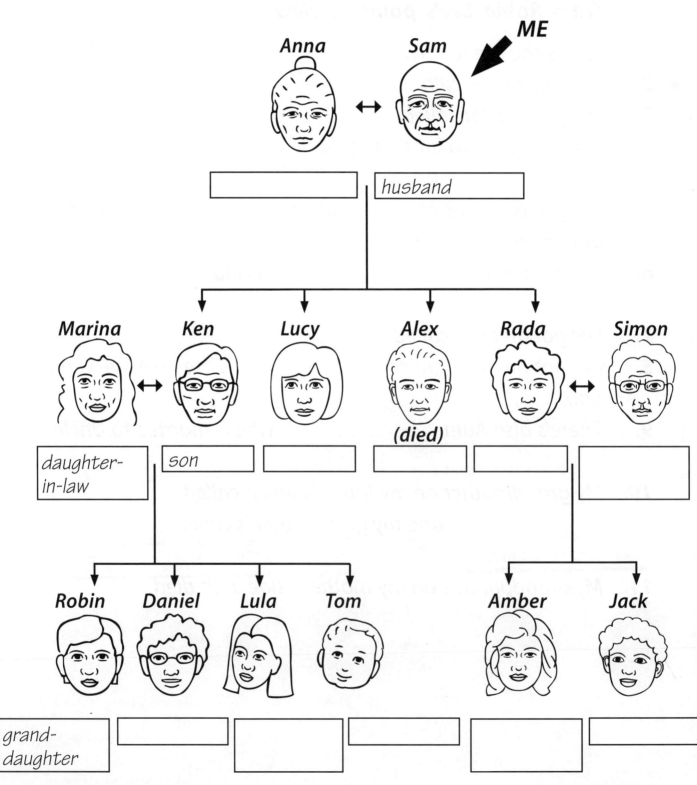

Family (4)

Sam Lee's Family Tree

Write about the family tree from Sam Lee's point of view.

1. This is the Lee family.
➡ 2. My name is _Sam_____.
3. I'm married. I'm the husband of _____. (Anna is my _____.)
4. We have 4 children - 2 _____ and 2 _____.
5. Our son, _____, is married to _____, our daughter-in-law.
6. We have a _____, Lucy, who is single.
7. Our other _____, Alex, died five years ago.
8. Our other daughter is _____, who is married to Simon, our _____.
9. Marina and Ken have 4 _____ - 2 _____ and 2 _____. Their names are _____, _____, _____, and _____.
10. _____ and _____ have 2 kids - a _____ called Amber and a _____ called Jack.
11. My granddaughters are _____, _____ and _____.
12. My grandsons are _____, _____ and _____.

spark workbook 4   page 35

Family (5)

Who are they?
Who is she/he?
Write the answers to the questions.

1.  This is my sister, Lucy.

➡ Who is Rada's sister?
➡ Rada's _____ is Lucy.

2.  This is my daughter, Amber.

Who is Simon's daughter?
Simon's _____ is _____ .

3. These are my parents, Simon and Rada.

Who are Jack's parents?
Jack's _____ are _____ and _____ .

4.   These are our children, Amber and Jack.

Who are Rada's and Simon's children?
Rada's and Simon's _____ are _____ and _____ .

Family (6)

Who are they?

Write the missing words about the family members.
Then write the sentences again in a different way.

▶ Anna's _husband_ is Sam.
▶ _Sam **is** Anna's husband._

➡ 1. Sam's _____ is Anna.
➡ _____

2. Anna's _____ are Ken, Lucy, Alex and Rada.
   Ken, Lucy, Alex and Rada **are** _____

3. Anna's and Sam's _____ is Marina.
   _____

4. Sam's _____ is Simon.
   _____

5. Ken's _____ are Anna and Sam.
   _____

6. Ken's _____ is Alex.
   _____

7. Ken's _____ are Lucy and Rada.
   _____

8. Ken's _____ is Marina.
   _____

spark workbook 4   page 37

Family (7)

Who are they?
Who is s/he?
Look at the answers. Make the questions.

➡ 1. <u>Who **are** Daniel's uncles</u>?
➡   Daniel's uncles are Alex and Simon.
2. <u>Who are</u>
   Daniel's aunts are Lucy and Rada.
3. <u>Who **is**</u>
   Amber's father is Simon.
4. _____
   Amber's mother is Rada.
5. _____
   Amber's brother is Jack.
6. _____
   Amber's aunts are Marina and Lucy.
7. _____
   Amber's uncles are Ken and Alex.
8. _____
   Amber's cousins are Robin, Daniel, Lula and Tom.
9. _____
   Amber's grandparents are Anna and Sam.
10. _____
    Rada's nieces are Robin and Lula.
11. _____
    Rada's nephews are Daniel and Tom.

Family (8)

What are they called?
What is she/he called? What is her/his name?
Write the sentences.

1. What is Rada's daughter called?
➡ Rada's _daughter_ is called Amber.

2. What is Rada's son called?
___

3. What is Amber's brother called?
___

4. What is Lula's grandmother called?
___

5. What is Lula's grandfather called?
___

6. What is Tom's brother called?
___

7. What are Tom's sisters called?
Tom's _____ are called _____ and _____ .

8. What are Tom's cousins called?
___

9. What is Lula's mother called?
___

10. What is Lula's father called?
___

11. What are Lula's cousins called?
___

spark workbook 4   page 39

Family Members

What order do they go in?
Copy these words in alphabetical order.

girl	boy	brother
grandfather	uncle	mother
child	wife	cousin
aunt	grandmother	father
daughter	partner	sister
nephew	grandson	niece
parent	husband	grandchild
son	sister-in-law	guardian

➡
- aunt
- boy
- b
- ch
- co
- d
- f
- gi
- grandc
- g
- g
- g

- g
- h
- m
- n
- n
- p
- p
- s
- s
- s
- u
- w

page 40

spark workbook 4

Male or Female

Are they male or female?
Copy the words from the last page in the correct places.

MALE	FEMALE
boy	girl

MALE and/or FEMALE

child

spark workbook 4

My Family

 How about you?
Draw your family tree.
Write about your family.

Dates (1)A

 When? Student A:
Read the missing dates with your partner and write them down in words. Then write them in numbers.

➡ 1. the sixth of March, two thousand and five
➡   6th March, 2005
➡   6/3/05

2. _____

3. the seventh of May, two thousand and six

4. _____

5. the second of October, two thousand and nine

6. _____

7. the sixteenth of August, nineteen ninety nine

8. _____

spark workbook 4

Dates (1)B

When? Student B:
Read the missing dates with your partner and write them down in words. Then write them in numbers.

➡ 1. _____
➡ *6th March, 2005*
➡ *6/3/05*

2. the fourth of December, two thousand and three
   _____
   _____

3. _____
   _____

4. the first of January, two thousand and one
   _____
   _____

5. _____
   _____

6. the ninth of July, two thousand and ten
   _____
   _____

7. _____
   _____

8. the nineteenth of September, nineteen ninety
   _____
   _____

Opinions (1)

How good or bad?

What do you think about it? How much do you like it? Read the words. Then write them in order underneath, from the best to the worst.

beautiful	terrible	great
not bad	really good	excellent
very bad	very good	OK
horrible	wonderful	fantastic
good	really bad	bad

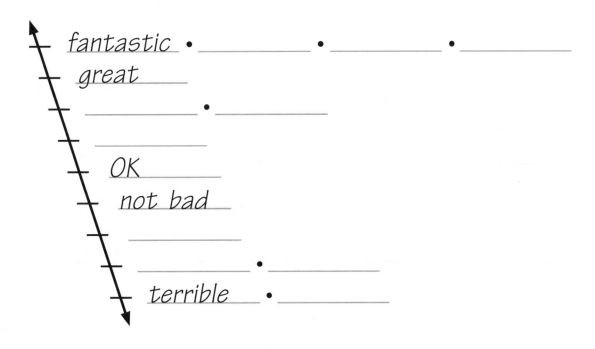

Opinions (2)

Word Search
Find the words in this word search.
(You can read them from the list on the next page.)

J	G	V	T	H	E	C	O	U	N	T	R	Y	M	H	V
J	E	A	N	S	H	O	U	T	I	N	G	C	N	V	V
Q	Q	O	M	T	T	M	C	C	A	R	R	O	T	S	C
Y	M	C	K	O	A	P	K	F	B	O	A	C	Y	N	I
R	Q	L	A	R	B	U	T	H	E	C	I	T	Y	K	H
C	G	K	K	M	L	T	H	E	S	U	N	H	V	F	H
V	R	A	T	S	E	E	L	T	H	E	B	E	A	C	H
W	A	T	H	E	T	R	A	I	N	P	O	W	U	M	W
X	A	P	P	L	E	S	X	B	E	A	W	O	S	H	T
K	S	Q	W	H	L	K	Z	C	A	R	S	R	T	S	E
D	O	I	N	G	N	O	T	H	I	N	G	L	R	W	B
F	I	G	H	T	I	N	G	P	N	F	B	D	A	M	H
V	V	L	S	Y	S	C	H	O	O	L	M	I	L	K	L
X	T	W	W	M	W	F	A	W	G	M	D	D	I	G	Z
B	Z	P	W	I	T	C	K	V	A	A	P	K	A	B	X
W	A	S	H	I	N	G	T	H	E	D	I	S	H	E	S

page 46   spark workbook 4

Opinions (3)

What do you think about them?

What do you think about it?
First, read the question, answers and list of words on this page. Then look at the next two pages.

▶ What do you think about _apples_ ?

▶ I (like)   it
    don't like (them) .

▶ I think it's _great_ .
        (they're)

What do you think about _apples_ ?

I _like them_ .
I think _they're_ _great_ .

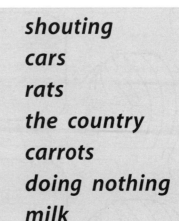

the sun	computers	shouting
storms	apples	cars
rainbows	the train	rats
table tennis	the city	the country
fighting	jeans	carrots
the world	school	doing nothing
the beach	Australia	milk
washing the dishes		

spark workbook 4   page 47

Opinions (4)

Choose 10 items from the last page, and make 10 questions. After that, ask your partner and write down the answers.

page 48

spark workbook 4

Opinions (5)

 Continue from the last page.

Opinions (6)

Write sentences about your partner.

▶ Tony _likes / doesn't like_ fighting.

▶ He / She thinks it's / they're really bad.

1.
2.
3.
4.
5.
6.
7.
8.
9.
10.

Opinions (7)

Now write sentences about yourself.

▶ I | like / don't like | _____ .

▶ I think | it's / they're | _____ .

1. _____
2. _____
3. _____
4. _____
5. _____
6. _____
7. _____
8. _____
9. _____
10. _____

The House (1)

What are they called?
Label the rooms and other parts of the house.

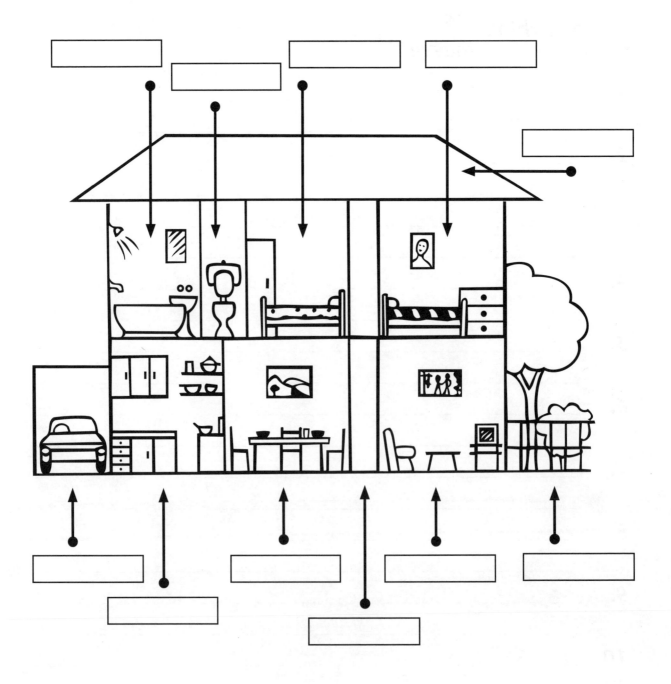

page 52

spark workbook 4

The House (2)

Fill in the missing words in these sentences.

→ 1. Inside the house, there are ☐ rooms.
→ 2. Also, there is a _garage_ outside, and a _____ with a fence outside.
3. The rooms are the 2 _____ **s**, the _____, the _____, the _____, the _____, and the _____.

My House or Flat
Describe your house or flat.

1. I live in a house / flat .
2. In my _____, there are ☐ rooms.
3. Also, there is a _____.
4. The rooms are the _____.

spark workbook 4   page 53

The Bedroom (1)

What is in the bedroom?
Label the things in the bedroom.

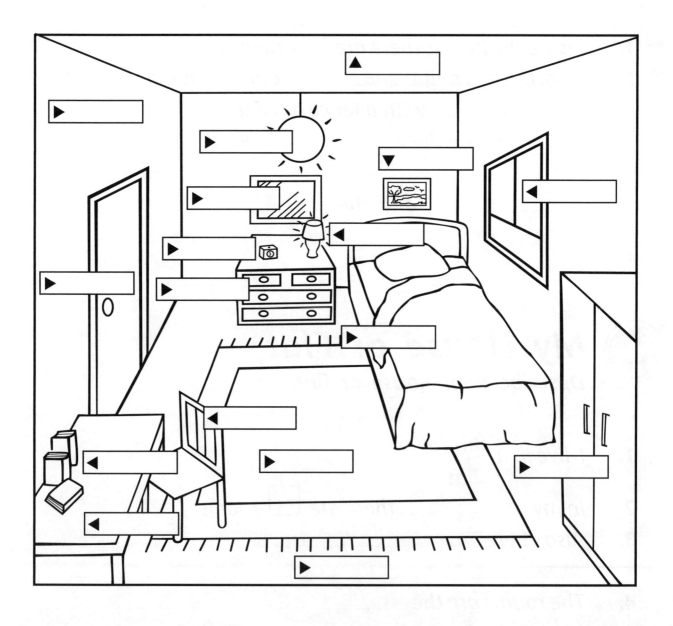

The Bedroom (2)

What colours?

Read these instructions and colour the picture of the bedroom.

1. Colour the bed red.
2. Colour the walls light blue.
3. Colour the ceiling white.
4. Colour the door light brown.
5. Colour the floor dark brown.
6. Colour the carpet red and dark blue.
7. Colour the cupboard yellow.
8. Colour the wardrobe yellow also.
9. Colour the table and chair grey.
10. Colour the lamp blue and pink.

Now write the missing colour words in these sentences.

➡ 1. The bedroom has 1 bed~~s~~. It is _red_ .
➡ 2. It has _light blue_ walls.
3. It has a _____ ceiling.
4. The door is _____ .
5. The floor is _____ .
6. There is a _____ and _____ carpet.
7. There is a _____ cupboard.
8. There is a _____ wardrobe.
9. The table and chair are _____ .
10. The lamp is _____ and _____ .

spark workbook 4   page 55

My Bedroom (1)

 What is in your bedroom?
Ask your classmates about their bedrooms.

	NAME				
1.	In your room, how many beds are there?				
2.	What colours are they/ is it?				
3.	What colour are the walls?				
4.	What colour is the ceiling?				
5.	What colour is the door?				
6.	What colour is the floor?				
7.	Is there a carpet or rug?				
8.	Is there a cupboard?				
9.	Is there a wardrobe?				
10.	Is there a table?				
11.	Are there any chairs?				
12.	What else is there?				

My Bedroom (2)

Make sentences describing your bedroom.

➡ 1. My bedroom has ☐ bed/s.

2. It is / They are _____ .

3. My bedroom has _____ walls.
4. It has a _____ ceiling.
5. The door is _____ .
6. The floor is _____ .

Make some more sentences in this way:

▶ There is / are a red and green rug .

➡ 1. _____
2. _____
3. _____
4. _____
5. _____
6. _____

Opposites (1)

What is the opposite?
Write the missing adjectives in the sentences.
(Look at the crossword puzzle to see if the words fit.)

1. _____ is the opposite of old.
2. _____ is the opposite of down.
3. _____ is the opposite of bad.
4. _____ is the opposite of right.
5. _____ is the opposite of tall.
6. _____ is the opposite of left.
7. _____ is the opposite of light.
8. _____ is the opposite of same.
9. _____ is the opposite of boring.
10. _____ is the opposite of big.
11. _____ is the opposite of old.
12. _____ is the opposite of slow.
13. _____ is the opposite of last.
14. _____ is the opposite of stupid.
15. _____ is the opposite of late.
16. _____ is the opposite of light.
17. _____ is the opposite of noisy.
18. _____ is the opposite of ugly.
19. _____ is the opposite of full.
20. _____ is the opposite of weak.
21. _____ is the opposite of fat.
22. _____ is the opposite of easy.

Opposites (2)

Crossword Puzzle
Now write the words onto the crossword puzzle.

Opposites (3)

What are they like?
What is he/she/it like?
Write the opposite words in the spaces.

1. The man isn't weak.
   ➡ He's _strong_ .
2. The homework isn't easy.
   It's _____ .
3. The car isn't slow.
   It's _____ .
4. The cup isn't empty.
   It's _____ .
5. The girl isn't quiet.
   She's _____ .
6. The mouse isn't big.
   It's _____ .
7. The book isn't boring.
   It's _____ .
8. The woman isn't young.
   She's _____ .
9. The flower isn't ugly.
   It's _____ .
10. The elephant isn't small.
    It's _____ .
11. The sun isn't dark.
    It's _____ .

Opposites (4)A

Student A:
Read the sentences with the missing adjectives with your partner. Together decide the answers.

➡ 1. The boy isn't stupid.
➡   He's _____ .
2. _____ .
   She's _____ .
3. The net isn't down.
   It's _____ .
4. _____ .
   She's _____ .
5. The shoes aren't the same.
   They're _____ .
6. _____ .
   He's on the _____ .
7. The computer isn't old.
   It's _____ .
8. _____ .
   He's _____ .
9. The answer isn't right.
   It's _____ .
10. _____ .
    It's _____ .
11. The woman isn't tall.
    She's _____ .

spark workbook 4   page 61

Opposites (4)B

Student B:
Read the sentences with the missing adjectives with your partner. Together decide the answers.

➡ 1. _____ .
➡   He's _____ .
2. The woman isn't last.
   She's _____ .
3. _____ .
   It's _____ .
4. The girl isn't fat.
   She's _____ .
5. _____ .
   They're _____ .
6. The man isn't on the right.
   He's _____ .
7. _____ .
   It's _____ .
8. The boy isn't late.
   He's _____ .
9. _____ .
   It's _____ .
10. The apple isn't bad.
    It's _____ .
11. _____ .
    She's _____ .

page 62   spark workbook 4

Places (1)

Write the names of the places, and choose the correct endings for the sentences.

1. You can go to the  _____ to _____ .

2. You can go to the  _____ to _____ .

3. You can go to the  _____ when _____ .

4. You can go to the  _____ _____ to _____ .

5. You can go to the  _____ _____ to _____ .

- ▶ catch a train
- ▶ buy some food
- ▶ go swimming
- ▶ you feel sick
- ▶ look at animals

Places (2)

 Continue making the sentences.

6. You can go to your _____ to

_____ .

7. You can go to the _____ to

_____ .

8. You can go to the _____ to

_____ .

9. You can go to the _____ _____ to

_____ .

10. You can go to _____ to

_____ .

- post a letter
- study
- go to sleep
- play football
- fix your teeth

Places (3)

Continue making the sentences.

11. You can go to the [bus stop] _____ _____ to _____.

12. You can go to the [ATM] _____ to _____.

13. You can go to the [library] _____ to _____.

14. You can go to the [cinema] _____ to _____.

15. You can go to the [river] _____ to _____.

- see a movie
- catch a bus
- read some books
- go fishing
- get some money

Places Game

Where do you want to go?

Each person puts a marker on START.
Throw a dice to see how many spaces to move.
The winner is the first person to get to FINISH.

- You want to buy some food. Go to the shop.
- You want to look at animals. Go to the zoo.
- You feel sick. Go to the doctor.
- You want to fix your teeth. Go to the dentist.
- START
- ZOO
- SWIMMING POOL
- Go forward 3 spaces.
- You want to play football. Go to the park.
- SHOP
- POST OFFICE
- You want to go swimming. Go to the swimming pool.
- You want to go to sleep. Go home.
- DOCTOR
- RAILWAY STATION
- You want to catch a train. Go to the railway station.
- HOME
- Miss a turn.
- RIVER

page 66

spark workbook 4

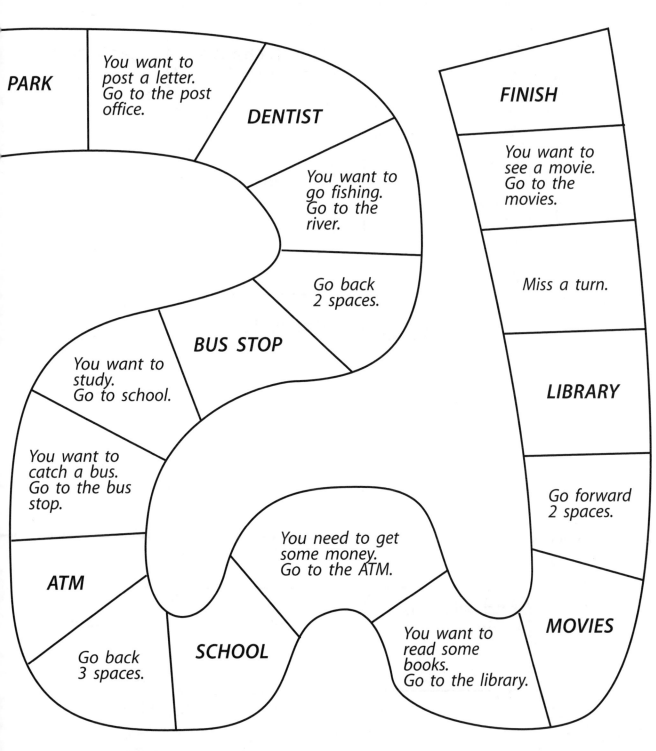

spark workbook 4

page 67

Address (1)

Fill in the missing words.

street	postcode	are
street number	suburb	town

Hi! How _____ you?

Hello! Good thanks. How about you?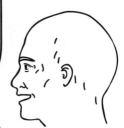

Good, thanks. Can you tell me which _____ or _____ you live in?

Garden Suburb.

And which _____ do you live in?

Rocky Road.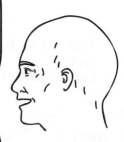

What is your _____ _____?

26.

And what is your _____?

6333.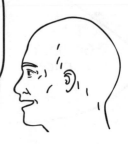

page 68   spark workbook 4

Address (2)

 Copy the questions.
Then ask your classmate, and write down the answers.

Forms

 Fill in the first form for yourself, and then ask your classmate.

Personal Information

Given name/s: _____

Family name: _____

Address:

    street number: _____ street: _____

    suburb/town: _____

    state: _____ postcode: _____

Personal Information

Given name/s: _____

Family name: _____

Address:

    street number: _____ street: _____

    suburb/town: _____

    state: _____ postcode: _____

An Envelope

 Write the name and address of your classmate on the front of the envelope.
Write your own name and address on the back.

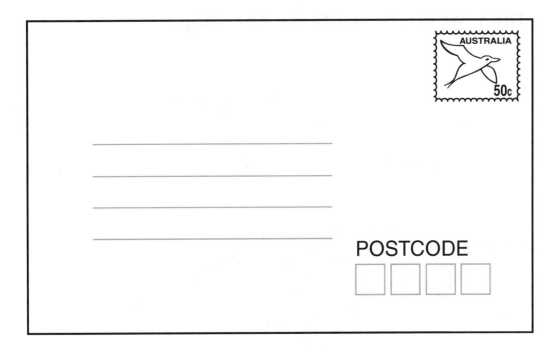

spark workbook 4

Directions (1)

How do you get there?
How do you get to the Oval?
Read the directions.
Then mark the route on the map.

1. Walk along Nerong Street until you come to Main Road.
2. Take a right turn into Helen Road.
3. Go along Helen Rd until it turns into John St.
4. Walk left along John Street.
5. The Oval is just on your right.

Directions (2)A

Student A:
How do you get to the park?
Read the directions to your partner.
Then mark the route on the map.

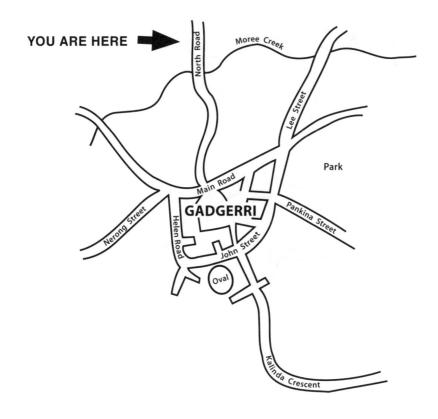

➡ 1. Go down North Road until you get to Main Road.
2. Turn left and go along Main Road until you get to Lee Street.
3. The park is just across the road.

Directions (2)B

Student B:
How do you get to the park?
Listen and write the directions your partner gives you.
Then mark the route on the map.

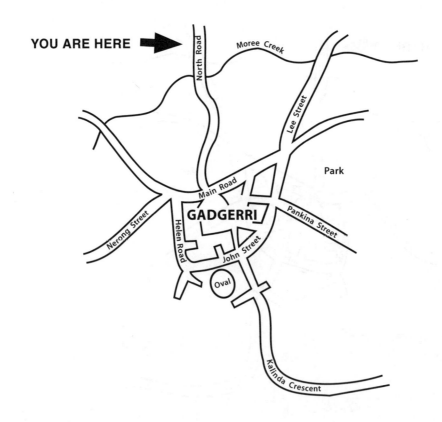

➡ 1. Go down _____ until you get to
   _____ .

2. Turn _____ and go along _____ until
   you get to _____ .

3. The _____ is just _____ the road.

page 74   spark workbook 4

Directions (3)A

Student A:
How do you get to Moree Creek?
Listen and write the directions your partner gives you.
Then mark the route on the map.

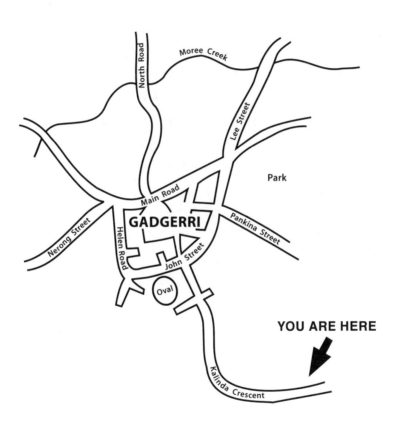

1. Go up _____ until you get to _____ .

2. Turn _____ and go along _____ past _____ .

3. Then you'll get to _____ .

4. Keep going straight ahead along _____ until you come to the _____ .

spark workbook 4 page 75

Directions (3)B

Student B:
How do you get to Moree Creek?
Read the directions to your partner.
Then mark the route on the map.

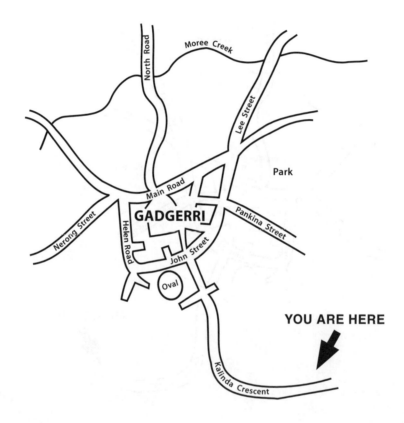

1. Go up Kalinda Crescent until you get to John Street.
2. Turn right and go along John Street past Pankina Street.
3. Then you'll get to Main Road.
4. Keep going straight ahead along Lee Street until you come to the creek.

Directions (4)A

Student A:
How do you get to the railway station?
Tell your partner and then mark the route.

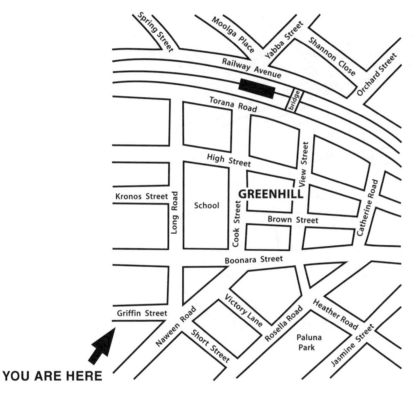

1. Walk right along Griffin Street until the corner of Naween Road and Long Road.
2. Turn left and walk along Long Road until the corner of Boonara Street.
3. Walk right along Boonara Street until Cook Street.
4. Go up Cook Street past High Street until you get to Torana Road.
5. Walk right to the railway bridge.
6. Go across the bridge into Railway Avenue.
7. The station is just on your left.

spark workbook 4   page 77

Directions (4)B

Student B:
How do you get to the railway station?
Listen and write, and then mark the route.

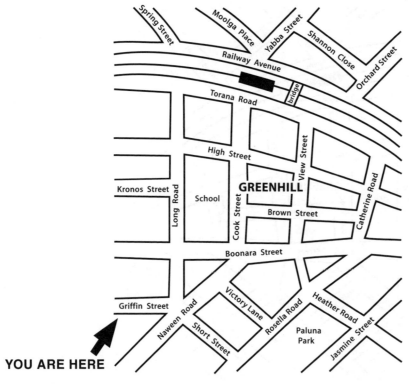

1. Walk _____ along _____ until the _____ of _____ and _____.
2. Turn _____ and walk along _____ until the _____ of _____.
3. Walk _____ along _____ until _____.
4. Go up _____ past _____ until you get to _____.
5. Walk _____ to the railway bridge.
6. Go _____ the bridge into _____.
7. The _____ is just on your _____.

page 78   spark workbook 4

Directions (5)A

Student A:
How do you get to the school?
Listen and write, and then mark the route.

1. Go along _____ until you come to the _____ of _____ .
2. Then turn _____ until you get to _____ .
3. From there, walk _____ until you get to _____ .
4. Go _____ along _____ until you come to _____ .
5. After that, turn _____ along _____ until you come to the _____ of _____ .
6. Finally, _____ the road into _____ and the _____ is just on your _____ .

spark workbook 4   page 79

Directions (5)B

Student B:
How do you get to the school?
Tell your partner and then mark the route.

1. Go along Jasmine Street until you come to the corner of Heather Road.
2. Then turn left until you get to Rosella Road.
3. From there, walk left until you get to Victory Lane.
4. Go right along Victory Lane until you come to Naween Road.
5. After that, turn right along Naween Road until you come to the corner of Boonara Street.
6. Finally, cross the road into Cook Street and the school is just on your left.

Places in Australia

 Write the missing words.

suburb	street number	world
postcode	city	town
state	states	country
street		

1. There are many countries in the _____.
2. Australia is a _____.
3. Australia has 7 _____ (if we include the Northern Territory).
4. NSW is a _____.
5. Sydney is a capital _____.
6. Greenhill is a _____ of Sydney.
7. Boonara Street is a _____.
8. 42 is a _____ _____.
9. 2999 is a _____.
10. Gadgerri is a _____.

Capital Cities

What are the capital cities?
▶ What is the capital city of <u>South Australia</u> ?
▶ The capital city of <u>South Australia</u> **is** <u>Adelaide</u> .
Make the questions and then write the answers.

1. capital • What • city • the • Australia • of • is • South

➡
➡

2. city • the • capital • Australia • Western • of • What • is

3. Victoria • capital • is • city • of • the • What

4. is • What • Tasmania • the • city • of • capital

5. What • of • is • the • New • capital • South • Wales • city

6. the • Queensland • capital • What • city • of • is

7. Northern • the • capital • Territory • city • of • What • is

8. capital • What • the • city • Australia • is • of

page 82   spark workbook 4

The Solar System (1)

 Label the planets in the Solar System, and also the Moon.

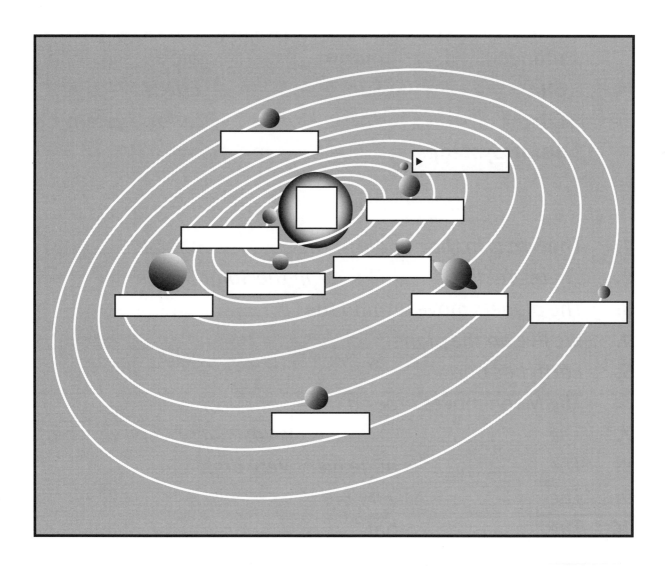

The Solar System (2)

 ## Describe the Solar System
Write the missing words in these sentences.

planets	moon	Moon
Sun	Sun	Earth
Earth	Earth	Solar System
Solar System		

1. The Sun is in the middle of the _____ _____ .
2. There are nine _____ in the Solar System.
3. The planets move around the _____ .
4. We live on the planet _____ .
5. Earth has one _____ .
6. The Moon moves around the _____ .
7. The _____ _____ is vast (very, very, very big).
8. The _____ is huge (very, very big).
9. The _____ is very big.
10. The _____ is big.

page 84   spark workbook 4

Lily Was Lucky! (1)

Write the missing words in Lily's story. Use the past tense for the verbs.

▶ paragraph 1:

➡ Yesterday morning I got up very late, at _____.

I thought I would be late for _____, so I did

everything very fast. I quickly had_____,

_____, _____,

_____, and _____.

▶ paragraph 2:

I finished getting ready after 30 minutes. It was nearly 8.20.

I knew a _____ would come at 8.22.

I only had two minutes.

spark workbook 4   page 85

Lily Was Lucky! (2)

 Continue writing the missing words in Lily's narrative.

▶ **paragraph 3:**

So I ran out of the house to get to the  _____ .

I saw the 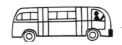 _____ come to the

_____ on the other side of the _____ .

▶ **paragraph 4:**

But the _____ was still red. I knew if I

couldn't catch that 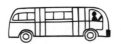 _____ , I would have

to wait 20 more minutes for another  _____ .

Then I would be late.

▶ **paragraph 5:**

So I didn't think about anything. I just ran. I crossed the

 _____ to the _____ when the

_____ was still red.

page 86   spark workbook 4

Lily Was Lucky! (3)

 Continue writing the missing words.

▶ paragraph 6:

But at the same time, a 🚗 _____ suddenly came around the _____ towards me. I tried my best to run quickly. The 🚗 _____ just touched my clothes and legs a little. It almost hit me! It was so dangerous. If I had been one second slower, I would have been killed!

▶ paragraph 7:

When I got on the 🚌 _____ , everyone was looking at me. I felt very silly. I knew it was a big mistake. My ♡ _____ was going very fast. When I got off the bus, my ♡ _____ was still beating quickly and couldn't go slowly.

Lily Was Lucky! (4)

 Finish writing the missing words.

▶ **paragraph 8:**

When I got to _____ , it was exactly _____ a.m. I was on time. I wasn't ~~early~~ late .

But I had almost lost my life!

▶ **paragraph 9:**

So now I promised myself I wouldn't go against the red _____ again. I would do it for my _____ and _____ - because they only have one child - and also for myself. Also, I will try to get up early ~~late~~ from now on!

page 88   spark workbook 4

Lily Was Lucky! (5)

Write out Lily's narrative. Continue on the next pages.
Change: **I** to **she**
  my and **me** to **her**
  myself to **herself**

▶ paragraph 1:
➡ Yesterday morning, **Lily** got up very late, at 7.45. **She**

▶ paragraph 2:

▶ paragraph 3:

spark workbook 4   page 89

Lily Was Lucky! (6)

Continue writing out Lily's story in paragraphs.

▶ **paragraph 4:**
➡ <u>But the traffic light was still red. She</u>

▶ **paragraph 5:**

▶ **paragraph 6:**

Lily Was Lucky! (7)

 Finish writing Lily's story.

▶ **paragraph 7:**
➡ *When she* _____

▶ **paragraph 8:**

▶ **paragraph 9:**

Lily Was Lucky! (8)

Present and Past Tense Verbs

Write the past tense verbs from the story.

VERBS	
PRESENT TENSE	PAST TENSE
get	
think	
do	
have	
eat	
brush	
clean	
finish	
is	
know	
run	
see	
cross	
don't	
come	
try	
touch	
hit	
feel	
isn't	
promise	

Lily Was Lucky! (9)

Past Tense Verbs

Write the past tense verbs in these sentences.

➡ 1. Lily _got_ up late.
2. She _____ she would be late for school.
3. So she _____ everything quickly.
4. She _____ a shower quickly.
5. She _____ breakfast quickly.
6. She _____ her hair and _____ her teeth quickly.
7. She _____ getting ready after 30 minutes.
8. It _____ nearly 8.20.
9. Lily _____ a bus would come soon.
10. So she _____ to the bus stop.
11. She _____ the bus coming.
12. She _____ the road.
13. She _____ think.
14. A car _____ around the corner.
15. She _____ to run quickly.
16. The car _____ her clothes and legs.
17. It almost _____ her.
18. She _____ very silly.
19. She _____ late for school.
20. She _____ herself to get up early now.

Shopping Game

What do you want to buy?

Each person puts a marker on START.
Use a dice to see how far to move.
The first person to get to FINISH is the winner.

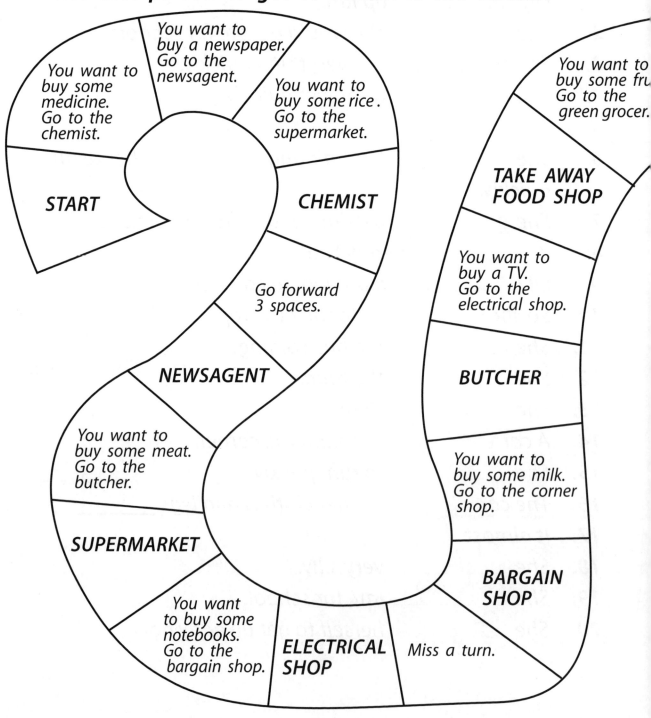

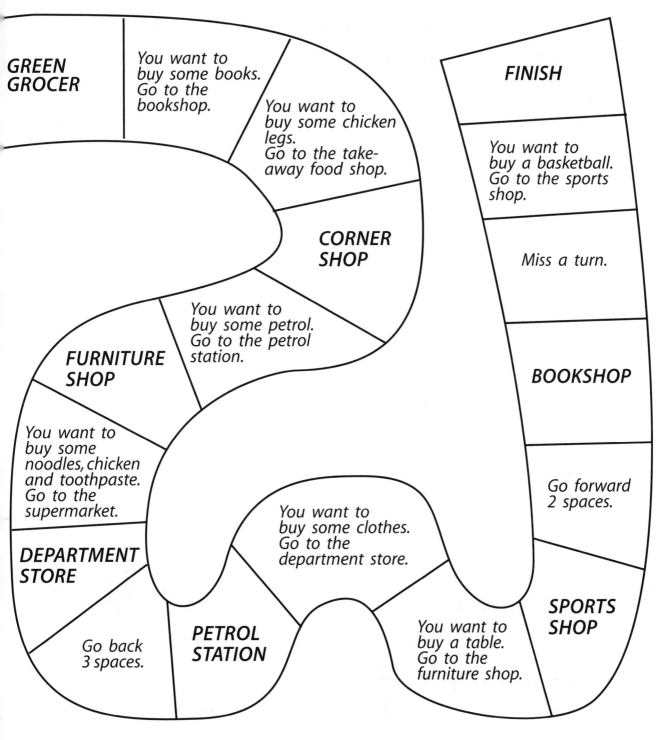

spark workbook 4 — page 95

Student Record of Achievement:

Name: _____

I have completed the work for the following topics:

- ☐ Feelings
- ☐ Favourites
- ☐ Classifying
- ☐ Things at School
- ☐ The Weather
- ☐ Family
- ☐ Dates
- ☐ Opinions
- ☐ The House and Bedroom
- ☐ Opposites
- ☐ Places
- ☐ Address
- ☐ Forms and Envelope
- ☐ Directions
- ☐ Places in Australia
- ☐ The Solar System
- ☐ Lily Was Lucky!
- ☐ Shopping Game

Date completed: _____